SACRED BLACK BLOOM

A Light-Bearer's Poetic Journey of Unfolding and Becoming

Jasmine L. Smith

Sacred Black Bloom: A Light-Bearer's Poetic Journey of Unfolding and Becoming

Copyright © 2025 by Jasmine L. Smith

Published by Solis Bloom Press

ISBN: 979-8-9927203-0-3

Paperback Edition
Printed in the United States of America

Cover & Interior Design by: Jasmine L. Smith

Disclaimer: This book is for informational and artistic purposes only. It is not intended to serve as a substitute for professional advice, therapy, or medical care. The author and publisher assume no responsibility for any outcomes resulting from the use of this book.

light-bearer
LITE-BEHR-ur
(noun)

A **Light-Bearer** carries wisdom, love, and truth—as a gentle glow, steady enough to guide rather than overwhelm. Their radiance emerges gradually, unfolding in subtle moments of growth, revealed in tender discoveries of who they truly are.

They move intentionally, honoring the past while softly illuminating the path forward. Rooted yet always stretching upward, they remind us that the light we seek isn't outside ourselves—it's already here, patiently waiting within.

Even in moments of rest, their glow remains.

Dedication

To my greatest blooms—my children

You are pure magic, wrapped in love, courage, and endless possibility. May you always trust that special spark inside you, dance to your own joyful rhythms, and remember that your journeys are beautiful adventures. I love you both beyond words—always, always.

To Black light-bearers—

Dreamers, healers, brave souls rising boldly, even from the heaviest soil: You carry forward the powerful legacy of those who came before you. Your resilience is honored, your journey profoundly valued. May these words affirm your power and celebrate your immeasurable worth.

To the light-bearers who have guided me—

For those no longer physically here, whose lessons and love remain, and those still walking this path beside me: You have given me clarity, comfort, and guidance. Your influence touches every part of my journey, and this work reflects my heartfelt gratitude for your lasting presence and love you've shared.

Dearest Light-Bearer,

Welcome to this unfolding journey. You hold more than words on a page—this is an offering, a sanctuary for reflection, renewal, and self-discovery. Within these pages, you'll find truths shaped by both shadow and light, words whispered from the heart, and soft invitations into stillness.

Throughout this poetic journey, you may notice phrases and words gently repeating. These repetitions are intentional, crafted to echo like affirmations, inviting you into a rhythm of reflection, remembrance, and renewal.

I honor your courage in picking up this book—in seeking reflection, healing, and a deeper understanding of your own unfolding. Like the Black Lotus, rooted in depths many fear, you hold within you a sacred power—blooming magnificently from conditions others might have thought impossible. The Black Lotus reminds us that growth is not linear, and even in our murkiest waters, we bloom in ways we never imagined.

Move through these pages as you feel called. Some words will resonate deeply—like old truths remembered. Others might softly invite you to meet yourself in a new light. May you recognize your strength, softness, moments of challenge, and profound triumphs. Allow yourself to rest in the stillness, reflect with openness, and bloom unapologetically.

You are part of a powerful lineage—a legacy of light-bearers who walked before you, and those who will follow the glow of your path. Trust the timing of your bloom. Honor the wisdom of your roots. Embrace the radiant light you were always meant to carry.

With love, light, and unwavering belief in your journey,

Jasmine L. Smith
Author of *Sacred Black Bloom*

Contents

The Journey

Closing Reflections

I carry sacred light, blooming even in the deepest waters

An Invitation to Begin

Stepping into your bloom

Take a deep breath, feeling your body to settle into this moment of stillness. Notice the calm rhythm of your heart and the supportive presence of the ground beneath you.

In this serene space, softly ask yourself:

What heaviness am I ready to set down?
What tender truth within me is now ready to take root and bloom?

Allow your reflections to flow freely onto the page—no judgment, no hesitation. Let your words spill gently, like seeds scattered in rich, welcoming soil. Wherever you find yourself right now—whether planting your first seeds of intention, quietly nurturing tender roots, or celebrating petals already opening to the sun—know that you are exactly where you need to be.

Pause here. Reflect deeply. Trust your unfolding journey.

The promise of becoming, in all its forms, begins with **intention.**

An Invitation to Begin: *A Creative Space*

Consider where you stand in your journey—perhaps you're planting your first seed, tending to delicate roots, or gently reaching toward the bloom ahead. Wherever you are, honor this sacred moment by visually expressing your growth. Draw, sketch, or craft symbols reflecting release, renewal, or unfolding strength. Allow creativity to unfold naturally, like scattered seeds finding their place in fertile soil.

I am planted with intention,
rooted in unwavering strength.

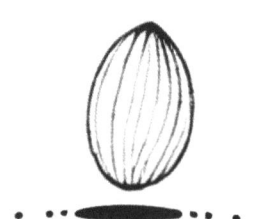

SACRED PHASE 1

THE SEED
The Quiet Promise of Growth

Where beginnings feel fragile
yet the unseen roots hum with quiet strength.
Honoring the wisdom of waiting,
the stillness that holds all things possible,
and the unseen becoming already underway.

The Seed Remembers

I am not small,
though my body fits between fingertips.

I am vast—a universe curled gently within, a galaxy compressed into a shell humming with songs of the infinite.

I am planted, wrapped in earth's embrace,
hidden not to disappear, but to ready myself.

Inside me lies a blueprint of my bloom—petals untouched by dawn, stems stretching skyward, roots holding firm through shifting waters.

Within me stir echoes of whispered prayers, rains that softened my edges, sunlight patiently tucked away.

There is no rush.

Subtle strength sleeps beneath my surface—patiently tempered, slowly gathering courage to delicately reshape what comes next.

Look closer—feel echoes of laughter ripple along my spine, rivers gently tracing paths beneath my skin, tiny worlds spinning lightly within my pulse.

The soil holds what I cannot yet see, but I trust the unseen roots are reaching—determined, calm, unshaken.

I am the seed,
complete even in shadows,
quietly prepared for the gentle unfolding ahead.

I carry everything I need to grow, even here

Reflection awaits on the next page...

Rooting Into Yourself

A grounding reflection

Close your eyes and imagine yourself as a lotus seed, nestled safely beneath serene, shadowed waters. Notice how gently the moisture seeps in, softening your outer shell with tender patience, quietly preparing you for growth.

In this gentle moment of anticipation, reflect:

As you remain embraced by the protective mud, what feelings softly rise within you—peace, restlessness, curiosity?

What quiet strength can you sense taking root inside you, anchoring steadily into the nurturing earth below, readying you for your ascent?

Allow your thoughts to flow freely, grounding you deeply into the present while opening pathways toward possibility.

Trust deeply in this truth: Just like the lotus seed, you already hold within yourself everything necessary for your blossoming journey ahead.

Rooting Into Yourself: *A Creative Space*

————◇——◇——◇————

Use this space to visually express the experience of resting beneath the surface, in the nurturing darkness of preparation. Through drawings, symbols, or abstract shapes, capture the emotions and energy building within, anchoring and preparing you for the journey upward. Allow your creativity to ground itself deeply and expand toward the possibilities ahead.

Black Soil, Sacred Ground

This soil is not barren.
It is not empty, not void.
It is rich, dark, alive;
the sacred ground
from which everything blooms.

Black soil,
carved by ancestral hands,
shaped by their melodies,
moistened by their tears.
I press my fingers deep,
feel earth cling softly,
cool and damp between my palms,
heavy with quiet strength.

It breathes stories—
resilience embedded,
a history refusing to fade.
Listen closely, and you'll hear
the subtle shift,
the faint hum
of roots reaching deeper.

Power thrives in its darkness,
brilliance quietly pulsing beneath.
Every grain infused with petrichor,
a fragrance heavy and earthy,
rich with ancestral whispers,
echoes of endurance,
the gentle assurance of growth.

This soil is ours.
It cradles us warmly,
nurtures us tenderly,
reminds us
we are not what they labeled us.
We are not dust;
we are life.

Black soil,
sacred ground,
home to seeds that flourish
through storms unseen,
through parched droughts,
bearing gracefully the world's heaviness.

From this earth,
we emerge—
unyielding, radiant, proud
Our roots grip history firmly,
our blooms stretch into endless tomorrows.

Let them witness:
How this darkness embraces
radiant potential.
How from fertile depths,
we raise forests,
cultivate gardens,
birth entire universes.

Black soil is sacred.
It is strength.
It is home.
It is us.

The Weight of Silence

The silence presses like gentle palms,
resting softly against my chest,
a subtle yet persistent touch.

It feels unfamiliar at first—
like mud cradling a seed,
like hands gently restraining me
when I long to run.

Yet silence is not emptiness;
it is hidden abundance—
a breath nestled deep within,
a heartbeat tucked into earth's embrace.

It is the soil
wrapping its arms around me,
tenderly binding me to restful surrender,
teaching me patience,
teaching breath as a slow dance,
fearless in quiet shadows.

I do not rush—
this sacred pause is shaping me,
carefully, from within.

The hush holds fullness;
it's where longing softens
and fibers awaken,
slowly stretching, sensing paths unseen

This is where beginnings stir—
underground, gathering the will to grow.

I am not buried here—
I am placed with intention.

This gentle pressure is not my enemy;
it is foundational—

a grounding touch that steadies me
as strength gathers beneath my skin.

In this breath-held moment,
I learn to trust
the patient unfolding
of becoming—
unhurried,
securely held.

The silence is weighty, yes—
but it carries me nearer to emerging light.

Even now,
this stillness sings
with the promise of bloom.

The Alchemy of Mud

Do not fear the mud.
It does not come to break you.

It clings not to drown,
but to anchor you within yourself—
to remind you:
there is knowledge hidden in its thick embrace.

The mud is sacred.
A womb where seeds awaken,
beginnings reach toward remembrance,
and where earth cradles life
into being.

It soothes the heat of memory,
loosens the soil beneath you
so your feet recognize where they belong.

It teaches that depth
is not defeat—
it is the starting place.

It coats wounds,
calmly, quietly,
an ancient balm whispering:
Be still.
This is how
the earth
mends itself.

(cont.)

Healing is not a sudden spark,
but a gradual unfolding—
growth nourished patiently
in places unseen.

The mud is not mess—
it is memory,
medicine,
presence.

Let it envelop you.
root you deeply.

Let it show you
how the effort you give now
will brace you, sure-footed
when it's time to rise.

The Drumbeat of the Roots

Beneath the soil, a rhythm awakens,
subtle and deep, timeless and true,
Boom-boom, boom-boom,
the pulse of roots,
the heartbeat of ancestors.

Do you feel it?
The earth hums with their stories,
through soles of feet planted firm,
through the vibration of soil
that remembers every step we've taken.

This is the song of those who came before,
a melody woven in dark loam,
their whispers resonant:
Grow strong.
Grow steady.
Grow together.

Roots do not rise alone.
They stretch toward one another,
braiding stories beneath the ground,
weaving softly across time
to hold hands in the dark.

We are one,
the roots say.

One pulse.
One rhythm.
One sacred lineage
that flows through the veins of the earth.

The drumbeat calls:
Do not forget.
Your resilience is ours,
your bloom is our celebration.

Listen.
The roots are drumming your name.
The land breathes in unity.
Ancestors rise in rhythm,
their voices woven with yours.

Boom-boom, boom-boom.

You are part of the song.
You are part of the whole.
You are the bloom they dreamed of.

My roots hold my strength, guiding me toward growth and possibility.

Reflection awaits on the next page...

Nourishing the Roots

Exploring what anchors you and what you're growing toward

Having explored the wisdom and nourishment found within the soil, pause now to reflect on your current place in your journey.

Imagine yourself as a seed, your roots extending deeply into the earth. These roots anchor you, providing resilience from your origins and holding the potential of your future growth.

This moment invites you to reflect thoughtfully on what has provided grounding in your life thus far and what aspirations you are reaching toward.

What to Do

1. My Anchor Points
On the left side of the page, write or illustrate what has anchored you—individuals, environments, experiences, or truths that have provided stability and support.

2. My Future Growth
On the right side of the page, note or sketch what you aspire to—goals, dreams, and new insights that are emerging, shaping your path forward.

3. The Center: Where I Am Now
In the center, at the intersection of your roots and branches, write one meaningful word or symbol that captures your current emotional or spiritual state.

See next page for exercise

My Anchor Points | **The Center:** | **My Future Growth**
Where I Am
Now

Roots of Home

I pressed my hands
into remembrance today,
felt grit of histories
beneath my nails—
scents of rain,
of fire,
of stories lived but rarely spoken.

This earth carries echoes—

Big Ma's voice humming gently
as her fingers shaped threads
into blankets holding quiet comfort,
Granny's laughter,
kitchen spices mingling with sweet joy—
my heart learning with each stir.

It feels Grandma's tender touch—
hands scented with soft flowers,
holding mine through playful afternoons,
through peaceful naps in sun lit
rooms that felt like home.

And it knows my mother's strength—
her voice clear,
firm,
shaping courage from uncertainty,
teaching me to bloom bravely
through unforgiving soil.

Their voices live here,
alive and present,
guiding me forward:

Ground deeply, child.
Even gentleness leaves its mark—
every lesson shapes.

Their truths anchor deeper into my bones.

Inwardly,
I promise to emerge—

for myself,
for dreams they planted,
for blooms they envisioned,
for the resilience of their stories
stitched lovingly into mine.

A Conversation with the Seed

I crouched in the soil,
hands cradling you,
a seed so small
I almost doubted
you could hold anything at all.

*What do you know
that I've forgotten?* I asked.
My voice trembled,
but yours was steady,
low and endless,
rising from the depths of the earth.

I know stillness, you said,
the art of lingering, unafraid.
Not every silence is absence;
some are sacred preparation.

I frowned.
But what if I don't bloom?
What if the dark swallows me whole?

You laughed, soft and warm,
like sunlight spilling underground.
You already carry the bloom.
It is not something you find;
it is something you remember.
Even buried,
your light cannot be dimmed.

But I feel lost, I whispered.
Small, unseen, forgotten.

(cont.)

You hummed,
your voice curling through the roots:
Lost is a word for those
who have yet to trust the journey.
Unseen is not forgotten,
and small is the size of beginnings.

I pressed harder,
my fingers sinking deeper into the bed of earth.
How will I know when it's time?

The same way I do, you replied.
The rain will soften you.
The sun will call you.
Your roots will know the way
without needing to see it.

I sat back, quiet,
listening to your wisdom settle.
And what should I do now?

Be here, you said.
Be still.
Grow unseen.
Trust that what feels like waiting
is already becoming.
You are not a question.
You are an answer
unfolding in time.

I held your words close,
their truth wrapping around my heart.

For the first time,
the silence felt less like an end
and more like a beginning.

The First Root

It begins with a crack—
a slow parting of what once held me whole.
The casing that sheltered me
now feels confined,
too snug for the promise
stirring beneath delicate skin.

A tremor moves through me,
bringing cautious questions:

What waits beyond this cocoon?
Will the earth welcome me,
or press against my tentative reach?

The first root pauses—
unsure, listening beneath the soil,
hesitant but reaching slowly,
uncertain, yet determined
to find a place in the dark.

Still, I press.

My first movement is subtle,
no louder than a breath,
like fingertips tracing new paths,
lightly carving paths into the unknown.

Each inch forward is a decision,
a vow whispered in shadow:
I will grow.

I cannot see clearly
what lies ahead—
yet something calls me forward.

To become,
I must shed the comfort of my shell,
embrace earth's heaviness,
and stretch slowly,
with trembling trust,
toward all I cannot yet know.

This is my beginning—
not born in boldness,
but in quiet courage
not with loud certainty,
but with a resilience that listens.

The first root reminds me:
growth is rarely grand at first.
It is measured, unfolding,
daring in its reach.

Even the smallest movement matters—
even the softest step forward
has strength enough
to split the earth open.

Unseen Ember

There is an ember
inside me—
faint,
but unwilling to fade,
alive in its waiting.

It does not blaze or blind,
nor plead for recognition.
It waits,
patient as dawn.

This glow is eternal,
older than my skin, older than my fears—
stirring beneath the surface,
a knowing nearly forgotten but never truly lost.

Even when buried,
it persists.
Even weighed down
with doubt and shadow,
it warmly reminds me:
I remain.

This spark is sacred—
a fragment of the first fire,
a shard of stars threaded into my bones.

It does not seek proof;
it simply is.

(cont.) 40

Below the earth,
it pulses softly—
like a heartbeat waiting to rise.

It is near—
it is home.
It may seem modest,
yet it holds the infinite.

When the moment comes,
it will awaken,
stretching toward the sun with a strength I've always held,
but only now trust to claim.

For now,
I honor its patience.
I trust its rhythm.
I carry its presence—
reserved in form,
unwavering in spirit.

Echoes in the Dark

In darkness,
their whispers surround me—
murmurs drifting
through shadow,
reminders
of who I am,
of confidence placed
carefully within my bones.

Their presence is familiar—
like memory,
like heartbeat,
intimate,
reassuring as breath.

They affirm:

You are held.
Our stories rest within you.
We journey alongside you
always.

In this darkness,
I listen deeply,
wrapped in their embrace,
presence like gentle fingertips
tracing my spine,
guided onward
by echoes
that speak my name.

The Seed's Intention

I look to the soil,
cradle of my becoming.

Guide me in patience—
to trust the dark,
to rest in quiet calm,
to know that growth
cannot be rushed.

Grant me courage—
to crack my casing,
to extend softly into the unknown,
to believe that the light
will find me.

Anchor me in certainty—
in the earth that holds me,
in the water that sustains me,
in the promise of a bloom
I cannot yet see,
grounding me gently,
as comforting as familiar hands
resting tenderly upon my shoulders.

I am rooted in trust and ready to embrace the growth that lies ahead.

Reflection awaits on the next page. . .

The Pause Before Growth

Honoring the stillness that nurtures your unfolding

Before stepping into your next phase, take a moment to pause—an invitation to appreciate and celebrate your journey thus far.

You have nurtured your potential, grounded your spirit, and embraced valuable insights. Rest intentionally in this moment, honoring the wisdom you've gathered.

Consider openly and warmly:

What truths emerged during your period of reflection?
How has rest prepared you for the growth ahead?
What feels ready to be gently released or welcomed as you move forward?

Take your time. Let your reflections move freely—like water naturally finding its path through earth. There's no need to rush; your growth is right on time.

The Pause Before Growth: *A Creative Space*

---◈---◈---◈---

This space is yours—an invitation to visually express the strength, growth, and vibrant energy you've cultivated. Draw, sketch, or create any symbol or image that resonates with where you are now, and where you're headed next. Trust your creativity, and let it unfold naturally. There's no right or wrong—only the joy of discovery and expression.

With each moment of growth, I root deeper and reach higher.

SACRED PHASE 2

THE SPROUT

Reaching for What Lies Beyond

Where the earth yields just enough
for new roots to stretch and take hold.
Honoring the courage to rise,
piercing the dense fog of doubt,
and trusting the first light, even before it is seen.

Through the Threshold

I am not your enemy, child—
I am your beginning.

I am the soil compacted around you,
the resistance that asks,
Are you ready?

You call me mess,
curse the way I cling to your feet,
pulling you downward
holding you steady—
but I am not here to bury you.

I hold you
to remind you
of your strength to rise.

Every sprout must push through something that grips, something that tests.

I've seen you curl inward—
muscles clenched, breathing shallow, pulse quickening with doubt.

Even then, I stayed—
not to trap you, but to teach you tension shapes your climb.

Now, you press back.

Now, you reach.

You split through the surface—
ease exchanged for memory in your veins,
power alive in every motion.

The mud doesn't yield easily.
But you move anyway.
And that movement is everything.

This movement is your marking—
a bloom carved through tension.

And when you lift from the deep, you carry more than roots.

You carry proof: you broke through.

Where the Light Enters

I used to hide the cracks—

masking the fissures where truth leaked through, afraid someone might glimpse
the fragile edges of who I am.

But hiding only deepened the ache, and shadows thickened, silent and
suffocating.

So, one day, I unsealed myself.
I revealed the fractures I'd hidden, the truths whispered only to darkness.

It felt raw, sharply vulnerable— yet fiercely liberating.

The very spaces I feared transformed into doorways, and warmth poured through
—softly, recklessly, flooding me with light.

This courage didn't shout.
It quivered quietly, exhaled uncertain breaths—
but remained open nonetheless.

Vulnerability was never weakness. It was the bravest choice I've made: allowing myself to be
fully seen, in the subtle strength of standing open.

I choose to stand open, honoring every part of me. In my openness, I welcome
the light.

Reflection awaits on the next page. . .

Inviting the Light In

A reflection on healing, strength, and vulnerability

Close your eyes and take a calming breath, settling into relaxation.

Visualize the spaces within you—not as flaws or gaps, but as doorways where fresh clarity can enter. These spaces hold purpose, offering insight and room to evolve.

Reflect on a moment when allowing yourself to be seen taught you something meaningful about who you are:

What realizations became clear through your vulnerability?
How did this moment shape your self-awareness or growth?

Write honestly, allowing your reflections to flow without judgment or expectation—like light moving freely into open spaces, illuminating what was previously unseen.

Inviting the Light In: *A Creative Space*

Use this space to visually represent what openness feels like for you. Sketch, doodle, or use symbols and shapes to capture the warmth, clarity, and insights that emerge when you invite understanding and growth into your life. Let your creativity flow freely—softly, boldly, or quietly—just like the light. Trust the shape it takes.

Roots in Still Waters

Before the stretch,
before the reach,
there is the sacred work of rooting—
a resilience
expanding in hidden spaces.

Below the surface,
where daylight does not enter,
I nestle into the depth below.

The cool soil curls around my roots,
damp and steady,
embracing me with earthen grace.

This is not stagnation—
it is deliberate preparation,
the patience of slow-moving rivers,
the knowing of seeds
waiting for their moment.

A slow current moves here—
water gliding calmly through roots,
breath easing within my chest.

Each root stretching downward
anchors me to truth:
to the subtle hum of the earth,
the songs of my ancestors,
the rhythm guiding my emergence.

(cont.) 62

I feel the mud's embrace,
no burden,
but grounding—
reminding me that to rise,
I must first belong to the deep.

Only by anchoring fully
can I touch the sky.

Only by trusting the still waters
can I gather strength to bloom.

Ancestral Roots

Their roots lift me,
hands gently guiding:

Step onward, child,
into your becoming.
The path ahead is clear—
your bloom awaits.

Their strength steadies me,
urging me higher,
teaching me where to reach,
how to unfurl.

I move forward,
sustained by their wisdom,
carrying dreams
passed tenderly
from their hearts to mine.

With every ascent,
I honor their voices,
their stories—
realizing the dreams
blending through generations,
embracing the horizon
they envisioned for me.

The Weight and the Bloom

I The Weight

It is heavy here,
under the surface,
where shadows press close,
and the earth feels too thick to breathe.

I carry echoes of silent battles,
the weight of hopes delayed,
and wounds that whisper
their ache beneath my skin.

Every step sinks deeper,
mud grasping,
suggesting surrender.

Here,
the light feels distant—
a fragile thread beyond my reach.

I feel my edges splintering—
almost breaking beneath it all.

Yet within these fractures,
something begins to stir.

II The Bloom

It is brighter now—
where shadows once held me.

(cont.)

The cracks that once weakened
have become doorways,
letting sunlight pour through,
restoring what I believed lost.

I ascend—
holding the weight lightly,
a badge of growth.

Each trial shaped my contours,
each tear fed hidden strength.
The earth that held me back
now supports my footing.

I stretch upward,
my spirit awake,
seeking sunlight.

Heaviness taught me poise;
the bloom taught me peace.

Together,
they authored my story:
a sacred unfolding,
a quiet reclaiming,
a glow born softly from shadows.

Between Water and Earth

There is a place where the water releases
and the earth receives—
a threshold between tides,
a pause between beginnings,
a haven for emerging.

Here, ancestral voices murmur,
like mist rising softly,
from depths only the spirit can touch.
Clay whispers secrets,
cool and smooth against fingertips,
a language felt rather than heard.

Time softens in this space,
where past gently blends into present,
and future stirs quietly in shadows.

This is the subtle edge of unfolding—
where breaking shifts into birthing,
steady, graceful, unhurried.

The river rinses lightly—
sorrow washed like sand,
old names drifting downstream,
carrying away what no longer fits.

The earth patiently holds me,
steady between currents,
supporting a shifting spirit,
a heart settling into rhythm.

(cont.)

Between water and earth,
I transform

I am seed becoming sprout,
root reaching bloom,
uncertainty blending into clarity.

I am tension and release,
movement within stillness—
the first breath of emergence.

No stars gleam here,
but their promise lingers.
No sunlight reaches,
but warmth courses through soil,
a memory that never left.

In this moment,
I surrender.

I press hands into clay,
letting its textures shape me,
to imprint wisdom
into hidden spaces.

And when I rise—
oh, when I rise—
I become river,
I become root,
I become light
born from quiet depths.

Soil Songs

The soil sings to me,
a hymn of resilience,
a melody of roots deepening,
of growth unseen but certain.

I rise, I reach, I root.
Through the mud,
I find my way—
through heaviness,
I discover my strength.

The soil sings softly:
You are stronger than storms,
yet gentler than rain;
you embody both,
and that is your power.

I rise, I reach, I root.
Each movement a rhythm,
each breakthrough a harmony.

The soil sings gently:
Bend, but do not shatter.
Stretch, but remain tethered
to the pulse beneath you.

(cont.)

I rise, I reach, I root.
With every crack in my spirit,
a new shoot emerges—
pushing upward,
embracing sun's song.

The soil sings steadily:
Child of the earth,
carrier of light,
you are the bloom we've awaited.

I rise, I reach, I root.

Fully alive in my becoming,
whole in my blooming,
anchored deeply in the song
of soil beneath my feet.

Grounded Wisdom

The mud shaped patience into my palms—
showed me how to rest,
even as heaviness pressed against my chest,
taught me to recognize that pausing
is not the same as defeat.

It pressed strength into me—
not the kind that yells or breaks,
but the kind that holds its shape
beneath pressure.

It nudged open my fingers,
helping me release
fears, shame,
the stories no longer mine to carry.

The mud softened,
letting slip from my grasp
all that no longer nourished,
leaving my hands ready
to hold what would.

It revealed beauty amid chaos—
the fragrance of earth after rain,
the texture of soil between fingers,
the subtle grace
of blooming despite uncertainty.

It taught me to listen—
to my breath,
to the whispers tucked into scars,
to the rhythm of healing
moving in its own time.

(cont.)

The mud taught me to glow—
by standing in the middle of the weight,
by finding the light
threading its way
through cracks and questions.

And when I rose,
I carried the mud's memory—
not as something to clean off,
but as something that shaped me
into who I've become.

The mud shaped me, but never limited me. What I learned there still feeds my roots.

Reflection awaits on the next page. . .

Harvesting Clarity

What the mud revealed

The mud—thick, unexpected, and often uncomfortable—may have held you longer than you anticipated. Yet within it, your roots deepened. Your resilience took form. Quiet truths rose to the surface.

Think back to a moment when life felt heavy or unclear—when you were asked to stay longer in the pause than you wanted to.

What began to shift once you stopped resisting and started listening?

Let your thoughts move gently through these invitations:

What truth revealed itself when everything else felt uncertain?
What quiet strength did you discover while moving through that space?

The mud doesn't define you. It deepened you.
Let this be your moment to name what grew.

Harvesting Clarity: *A Creative Space*

Take this moment to reflect on the lessons life's messy moments have offered you. Through symbols, colors, or shapes, create a visual representation of your journey through the mud—not just the weight you've carried, but the roots you've grown and the light you've found.
Let this page hold your growth, your resilience, and the wisdom you've gathered along the way.

The Choice to Rise

The mud is both weight and womb,
both anchor and awakening.
It pulls at my ankles,
tests my breath,
whispers:

Stay.

And I could.
I could surrender to heaviness,
call it rest,
call it shelter.

But settling is not my nature.

There is fire in my marrow,
a rhythm in my bones
that beats louder than doubt.

The earth grips me,
textured and persistent—
not as a cage,
but as a gentle challenge:

Will you move?

Every step forward
is a defiance.
A breath taken anyway.
A choice made again and again.

My roots do not restrict—
they anchor me to origins,
a soft reminder of strength,
of where I first grew.

Inner voices quietly remind me:
You carry growth inside,
you extend beyond this moment.

I embrace the stretch,
the tension,
the upward pull.

Each motion a subtle uprising,
each breath a returning melody.

I rise—not easily,
but purposefully.
Because within, I sense clearly:
what awaits above this shadow
is richer than all I leave behind.

Shadows and Sunlight

I The Shadows

In the shadows, I am unsure,
a silhouette pressed against the earth,
carrying doubt like a second skin.

Whispers of *not enough*
coil around my thoughts,
thick as mist,
cool and lingering at dusk.

Darkness slows my steps,
making each movement hesitant,
each hopeful thought a distant murmur.

Here, my identity blurs.
Here, my inner fire dims.
The world contracts to silence,
and I question
if I'll ever step beyond this heaviness.

II The Sunlight

The light meets me quietly—
even through narrow openings,
beneath layers of weight.

It speaks in golden tones,
calling my name back to me,
lifting the fog from my spirit.

I reach toward its touch,
softening at its presence,
breathing deeper, easier.

(cont.)

The sunlight reminds me:
I am not only the shadows.
I am the dawn breaking through them.

Each doubt becomes a stepping stone,
each ache a map toward healing.

The shadows taught me resilience;
the sunlight shows me joy.

Together, shadow and light
compose my journey—
a balance of dusk and dawn,
a soul that never surrendered to darkness.

Now, I carry both within me:
the depth of shadow,
the brilliance of sunlight.

And still,
I shine —
steady,
grounded,
whole.

In the balance of shadows and sunlight, stillness becomes the bridge to growth.

Reflection awaits on the next page. . .

Discovering Stillness Within

Finding clarity and renewal in moments of quiet reflection

You've traveled through the mud—moments of heaviness, grounding, and quiet—and grown in resilience and understanding. Before moving into the Budding phase, pause here, honoring the stillness you've cultivated.

Consider what inner strengths emerged from this restful period.

Name how the mud has grounded you, nourished your growth, or prepared you for the steps ahead.

Explore which part of yourself now feels ready to gently open toward new possibilities.

Celebrate the progress you've made, honor the restful growth you've embraced, and warmly anticipate the beginnings awaiting you.

Discovering Stillness Within: *A Creative Space*

◆——◆——◆

Use this space to honor the gentle resilience you've found. Draw, write, or use colors and symbols to express what stillness feels like to you. Let your expression be soft or bold, delicate or wild—whatever feels true. There's no right way to capture this moment. Simply create, and let your quiet strength take shape on the page.

I unfold at my own pace, nourished by both stillness and growth.

SACRED PHASE 3

BUDDING

Bridging the In-Between

Where the edges soften
petals pressing forward, uncertain yet unafraid.
Honoring the beauty of in-between,
the surrender to motion,
and the knowing that unfolding has already begun.

The Surface Calls

The roots hold my story—
every scar, every shadow,
threaded deep beneath the surface.

I have rested in solitude,
wrapped in patient strength,
learning the rhythm of my becoming.

Now the surface calls—
an invitation,
not a summons.

I rise,
carrying the ground within me—
its whispered truths, its earthy grit,
living evidence of endurance.

The earth yields gently,
perfume of rain-soaked soil lingering,
like a slow exhale,
like mist softly rising from the meadow.

The light meets me,
its warmth reminding me
that readiness is not perfection—
it is presence.

I am whole in this moment—
shaped by all I've carried,
ready now to unfold
into the fullness awaiting me.

Pierce the Surface

The surface seemed unbreakable—
a barrier of doubt,
a heaviness of fear,
layers pressing me down,
murmuring, *Not yet. Not you.*

But today,
the sprout found its way through,
guided by gentle persistence,
by a steady knowing within—
I had always belonged to sunlight's embrace.

Roots held firm in the unseen—
intertwined in subtle strength,
nourished by shadows
that softened my sharpest edges
and whispered, *Keep going.*

And as I stretched upward,
the weight became memory.

The barrier that once seemed endless
opened like a sigh.

Now I reach for the sun,
its warmth—
an anthem to my becoming.

Each leaf unfurls with purpose,
each breath sings clearly:
I am here.

Today,
the sprout broke free—
pushing through doubt,
rising from hesitation,
moving beyond boundaries
with a courage bold enough
to meet the sun.

The Mosaic of Me

These pieces I carry
were never broken—
they were shaping.

Each fragment, each edge
a moment I lived through,
crafted intentionally
by what I overcame,
colored by truths
I discovered along the way.

I once hid my scars,
believing the cracks
marked me incomplete.

Yet healing revealed
imperfection's radiant geometry—
each flaw a facet,
each edge a reflection.

Now, each piece fits naturally
beside the others,
held securely
in gentle alignment—
a careful artistry,
binding my story
into something whole.

(cont.) 92

This mosaic
is no longer a question,
no longer a wound—
it is strength,
reclaimed and cherished.

Every line matters.
Every mark shines.
Every moment, integrated,
has made me
who I proudly am.

I stand,
fortified by all I've learned,
anchored by each challenge I've endured,
as I journey home to myself

I honor every piece of my journey, for it has made me whole.

Reflection awaits on the next page. . .

Embracing All Parts of Yourself

See yourself as a mosaic of wholeness, beauty, and authenticity

Take a moment to sit comfortably. Close your eyes and breath deep—inhaling peace and exhaling any lingering stress.

With each breath, allow your imagination to guide you.

Picture yourself as a mosaic—a beautiful work of art composed of many unique pieces. Each fragment holds its own shape, color, and texture. Some pieces shine brightly, others hold shadows, yet together they create a meaningful and complete image.

Reflect on a part of yourself you've found challenging to embrace:

How have you learned to welcome and include this part of you, fostering wholeness and deeper understanding of yourself?

When you're ready, open your eyes and write openly. Describe your mosaic with appreciation and kindness, honoring each piece of your authentic self.

Embracing All Parts of Yourself: *A Creative Space*

You are a mosaic—a masterpiece crafted from every piece of your life. In the space below, draw, write, or sketch your mosaic. Use shapes, colors, or words to represent the textured pieces of your story—the experiences that stretched you, shaped you, or called you to grow. Include the smooth, radiant pieces that reflect your joys, strengths, and triumphs. Let your creation become a celebration of your wholeness—a reminder that every piece belongs.

Inhale of Light

At first, it was a shimmer—
barely there,
a radiance brushing the edge of my awareness.

I didn't reach for it.
It arrived—
slow,
steady,
settling across me like morning.

The darkness hadn't vanished.
It softened,
creating space for something new to enter.

And when it did,
it felt like breath
after a long forgetting.

No blaze,
no sound—
just the still air shifting,
and something inside me answering.

The soil still clung to my skin.
The ache hadn't disappeared.
But my chest expanded,
breath easing open.

This was the moment
I felt myself
welcomed into the light.

No proving. No striving. Only presence.

Only this breath—
and all it carried forward.

Shedding the Weight

Shame draped me like a heavy cloak,
clinging, unwilling to let go.

It whispered in the quiet,
rooted in hollow spaces where I once held myself too tightly.

I shrank beneath its presence—
mistaking heaviness for comfort,
its hold for home.

But even seeds must split open,
the sprout must press against the soil.
And the lotus must rise through water before it can bloom.

So I loosen my hold on shame—
releasing it with trust,
letting it crumble like dry leaves,
crumbling into sweet, damp earth
where it softens, transforms,
becoming the foundation
that steadies me.

I stand taller now,
my breath lighter,
my spirit unfolding toward the light.

No longer
afraid of being seen—

for I know now,
I am worthy
of being known.

The Light Within

Deep in the silence of my being,
beneath layers of fear and forgotten dreams,
an ember began to stir—
small as a whisper,
steady as an ancient truth.

It glowed like a lantern,
casting shadows into stories,
turning doubt into echoes
that softened with each breath.

This flame was not borrowed,
not given, nor taken.
It was mine—
a spark sown in the fertile soil of my soul.

I felt it awaken,
warmth seeping through old wounds
its flicker weaving strength from every tear,
every triumph.

The lotus of my spirit rose,
breaking the surface with quiet resolve,
a beacon unshaken by ripples,
holding the sun in its petals
and the stars in its reflection.

I am the flame I have nurtured,
the lantern I have tended.
I am the ember,
the spark,
the glow.

This light is mine.
It always was.
And it grows brighter
with every breath,
every truth,
every step forward.

Echoes of the Journey

I carry the echoes of storms—

their thunder once roared,
shaking the roots of my being.

Now they move through me—
a quiet vibration,
seeping into the tender spaces,
a reminder
of paths I've traveled.

The shadows that once stretched long,
looming over my every step,
have melted into dusk—

no longer a threat,
but a memory that whispers:

You are still here.

Each drop of rain
that touched my spirit,
each wave
that coursed through me,
rests now
within the well of my soul—

not as burden—
as evidence I grew,
as proof I endured,
as the intricate truth carved into my spirit.

(cont.)

The weight of water
taught me to float.

The stillness of challenge
taught me clarity.

Marks upon my heart
revealed beauty
in every line of my story.

I honor the journey
that sculpted me—
the winds that shifted my path,
the shadows that refined my glow.

Every step
brought me here—
to understanding,
to quiet power,
to authenticity.

Echoes remain—
not as anchors,
but as song—

a melody of resilience,
carried tenderly,
in celebration.

Emerging from the Dark

Beneath the surface,
the shadows lingered—
still and patient,
wrapping their whispers around my heart:

You are not enough. You will not rise.

I paused at the threshold—unsure if I was ready to step forward.
Their presence clung tightly, turning movement into hesitation,
turning hope into a distant flicker.

I felt cold whispers
sliding across my skin
darkness extending,
their touch weaving into places I once tried to bury.

Yet, relentless sunlight found me—
pouring through subtle cracks,
its pull stronger than my fears,
its truth dissolving doubt.

I push beyond the threshold,
breaking free from shadowed whispers,
persistent beams of sunlight
tugging me firmly upward.

(cont.) 106

Darkness loosened,
not erased—reshaped,
now an intricate part of my strength.

What once held me tightly
became the roots anchoring my growth.

The scars they etched became storylines,
evidence of courage rather than damage.

I step forth deliberately,
each movement a beautiful rhythm—
present, determined, and ready for the sun.

This is my emergence—from burden to balance,
from shadowed hesitation to steady certainty.

A Love Letter to Myself

Dear Me,

I see you.
In every tender moment of doubt,
in every quiet triumph,
in the spaces where you thought
no one noticed—
I see you.

You are more than your accomplishments.
You are not defined by what you give,
nor by what you carry alone.

Even in uncertainty, you remain enough.
Even in stillness, you are worthy.
Even when you feel dim,
there is light inside you that never fades.

I honor the way you've grown—
roots gripping the soil of resilience,
branches reaching toward possibility,
even when the sky seemed far.

I know there were moments
when you forgot your strength,
when you doubted your voice.
I know you gave your light away
to those who couldn't see it.

But still—you endured.
You found a way to keep going,
to keep breathing,
to keep blooming.

I celebrate the moments you chose yourself—
your joy, your healing,
your beautiful, sacred truth.

You are both the scar and the strength,
the wound and the wisdom.
You are every lesson lived,
and every dream waiting to unfold.

And you are loved—deeply, endlessly,
by the person who knows you best.

With gratitude and grace,
I promise to carry you gently,
to speak your name with kindness,
to hold your heart as my own.

Because it is.
Because you are.
And because you always will be—
a masterpiece in progress,
a light that never fades.

With all my love,
Me

My light shines brighter because it carries the wisdom of every shadow I've
known.

Reflection awaits on the next page. . .

A Love Letter to Myself

Holding space for your own story

Find a quiet space where you can be still. Close your eyes and take a deep breath, allowing yourself to settle into the moment.

Recall a time when things felt uncertain or challenging, yet you chose to move forward anyway. Hold this memory—not to judge it, but to honor the courage and compassion you showed yourself during that time.

Reflect warmly on how this experience shaped who you are now: How did it influence the way you see yourself? What inner strengths or qualities did it help you recognize?

When you're ready, **write a heartfelt love letter to yourself:**

Thank yourself for showing up, even when it wasn't easy.
Acknowledge and appreciate the beauty in your complexity—both the light and the shadow.
Celebrate your courage, kindness, and all the ways you've shown compassion to yourself.
Make a thoughtful promise—a caring intention—for how you will continue to support and nurture yourself along your journey.

Let your words flow openly and sincerely, holding space for your own story—honoring every part of who you've been, embracing fully who you are now, and welcoming the person you are becoming.

The Strength to Rise

My roots run deep,
anchored in the mud that once sought to hold me—
its weight a reminder
of storms I've weathered,
doubts I've answered bravely,
and whispers of *you can't*
met by reaching upward anyway.

I am neither fragile nor fleeting.
I am the stem stretching skyward—
my tension a hymn of endurance,
each inch of growth declaring softly:
I will rise.

The sunlight touches me,
its warmth a reassuring guide,
brushing past the lingering shadows,
its whisper constant:
You were always meant to grow.

With each heartbeat,
I ascend—
moving with trust, never rushed,
each gesture carved from wisdom,
each root gently affirming the resolve it takes to thrive.

I stand for those who came before me,
their courage vivid and flourishing in my veins,
their resilience braided through my spine.

I carry their brilliance—
unshaken, unwavering,
a quiet force shaped and nurtured by earth and memory.

This is my power:
embracing every fracture as fertile ground,
choosing to lift myself higher.

Here I am—
grounded yet rising,
embodying tenacity like never before.

This Is My Light

This is my light—
not borrowed, never dimmed,
but born from quiet embers
ignited by each moment
I chose to keep moving forward.

It carries the splendor of countless stars
collected tenderly in my name,
a constellation of bravery
softly etched into my spirit.

It is the lantern I have carried,
its illumination soft yet constant,
a subtle companion
through shadowed nights.

This is my light—
subtle, persistent,
a glow refusing to fade,
offering solace to all who seek.

It cannot be dimmed
by whispers of fear
or shadows of expectation.
It shines because I exist,
because I breathe,
because I believe.

I claim it wholeheartedly,
its warmth my refuge,
its brilliance my truth.

This is my becoming:
I am the ember.
I am illumination,
I am the light itself.

The Horizon Beckons

The horizon hums,
a melody felt before it's heard—
an invitation to expand,
a gentle pull toward openness.

It marks a beginning,
a spaciousness ready to embrace
all that I am growing into—
rooted, flourishing,
opening endlessly.

The lotus rests gently on tranquil waters,
its bud softly stirring,
waves whispering at its edges—
a rhythm grounding,
patiently encouraging it open.

Above,
the sky stretches boundlessly,
hues merging with dreams unspoken,
its glow gently beckoning me upward.

I pause,
content in this restful moment—
roots steeped in truths from deeper waters,
buds gently awakening to possibilities.

Yet the threshold calls,
igniting readiness,
a quiet certainty within.

I move forward—
breath blending with wind,
spirit reaching toward expansive skies.

I carry my journey—
each bud holds a heartbeat,
each line a lesson learned,
each breath affirming:
I am continuously preparing,
reaching,
and evolving.

Emerging signals a sacred pause,
a moment honoring the path traveled,
before embracing what lies ahead.

The horizon waits,
arms open,
its voice tender:
Come. There's more beauty awaiting you.

I step toward the horizon with trust, carrying the light of all I've become.

Reflection awaits on the next page. . .

Illuminating the Path Ahead

Carrying the light forward

The horizon calls—not to hurry you, but to warmly welcome you forward.

Close your eyes and take a deep breath, noticing the warmth gently expanding within you. With each inhale, welcome a sense of clarity and reassurance; with each exhale, release lingering uncertainty.

Imagine yourself standing at the horizon's edge, where earth meets sky. Behind you is the road you've traveled—the experiences you've had, what you've learned, and the ways you've grown. Ahead is your path forward, brightened by your own inner light.

In this moment, reflect:

What quality or insight from this budding phase do I most want to carry forward as I step intentionally toward my bloom?

When you feel clear and ready, craft your affirmation with intention. Begin your words:

"With my light, I will intentionally..."

Let this affirmation ground and support you, signaling your readiness for the beauty that awaits..

With my light, I will intentionally . . .

I expand with confidence, radiating my truth with clarity and grace.

SACRED PHASE 4

BLOOMING

Opening Fully into Self

Where hesitation fades into certainty
and petals stretch wide in the sun's embrace.
Honoring the fullness of self,
the grace of standing whole,
and the power of being seen, unhidden and
unashamed.

The Light That Found Me

There was a time I hid from mirrors,
afraid of what they might reveal—
a shadow of myself,
a flicker lost in the fog of trying to be enough.

The light found me in its own way—
not rushing in like fire,
not crashing down like thunder,
but soft and patient,
lingering just beyond my doubt.

It slipped in silently,
tracing pathways through spaces I overlooked,
pouring warmth through hollow places within me,
awakening something I had long forgotten:
my reflection.

It waited—
steady, resolute—

until I dared to turn toward it.

Each shadow I faced
fed the roots of my becoming,
each opening widening just enough
for radiance to seep inside.

In its brightness,
I saw myself clearly—
whole in tenderness,
strong in softness,
worthy even in my uncertainty.

(cont.) 124

The light had always been mine—
buried beneath layers of hesitation,
silently expanding within spaces
I once believed were empty.

Fortified by stillness,
cultivated in silence,
it waited for me to trust its existence.

Now—
this light moves through me,
a quiet glow steady in the wind,
fully ready to be seen.

I embody this radiance,
guiding each step,
filling each breath,
illuminating every truth I claim.

The light found me.
And when I met its gaze,
I found myself.

I trust my radiance; my light is uniquely mine.

Reflection awaits on the next page. . .

Claiming Your Light

Embracing the radiance that was always yours

Close your eyes and breathe deeply.

With each exhale, picture the gentle radiance within you growing clearer, warmer, brighter—expanding effortlessly into the space around you.

Now, complete these affirmations:

My light is _____.

My light grows when I _____.

My light inspires me to _____.

Allow your responses to emerge naturally. Consider this moment an invitation to fully embrace your truth, openly declaring the radiance uniquely yours.

My light is

My light grows when I

My light inspires me to

Where the Lotus Rises

I began in the depths,
where waters ran murky,

where weight settled heavy
and gritty like silt.

A silent promise lived within me,
planted deep—
waiting patiently to rise.

The sun felt distant,
a rumor carried softly by ripples.

Yet even in darkness,
my roots pressed onward—

weaving through shadows,
digging past uncertainty,
searching for warmth
I could not yet touch.

Each experience brushed against me,
softly revealing new layers within.

Moments I gathered
shaped my growth,
anchoring me gently
in who I was becoming.

(cont.)

Slowly,
I emerged—

through currents of hesitation,
through shadows that clung,

stretching toward a brightness
I had never touched,
but always believed in.

Then—
I broke the surface.

The world opened before me—
sky blooming with infinite promise.

The bud I once protected
now unfurled wide beneath sunlight,
tender yet sure.

My roots remain deep,
a quiet echo
of my beginning.

But here,
my petals now open gently,
embracing sunlight above the surface.

this is where the lotus rises.

Radiant and Rooted

I am the bloom of every dream,
sown in the soil of resilience,
holding the patient promise of blossoming within me.

Nourished by whispered prayers, delicate as mist,
I broke through the earth,
my roots embracing memory,
my petals unfolding with subtle courage.

I did not rush.
I grew in stillness first—
learning patience from the soil,
trust from the rain,
and strength from the winds that bent me,

but did not break me.

Before my petals opened,
I discovered power in pause—
recognizing waiting as wisdom,
never weakness.

Now I stand—radiant and rooted,
grounded in my beginnings,
reaching steadily for what lies ahead.
My strength intertwined with my tenderness—
steady, assured, complete.

I carry the comfort of prayers murmured in darkness,
and the clarity of lessons shaped by shadow.

I am a light that endures through shadow,
a foundation rebuilt through every tremor.

Each breath sings of subtle triumph,
each step affirms my growth.

I am radiant.
I am rooted.
I am the bloom of every dream
brave enough to rise beyond the earth.

Flame in the Bloom

There is fire in this bloom—
vibrant in every petal,
smoldering within my bones,
alive in every breath, every heartbeat.

I used to fear this heat—
worried it might unravel me,
turn me to ash
before I learned to stand.

But my body remembers
the language of embers.
It knows this heat rises
to awaken, to reveal.

I no longer shield myself
from this warmth
prickling at my edges,
ignited when my truth meets sunlight.

I stand fully
in this embodied blaze,
letting it ripple through my veins,

fueling every step,
every bold unfolding.

This inner fire surpasses metaphor—
it is breath, blood, bone.
A living force, fierce and clear,
illuminating my way
as I move boldly
toward the sun.

Lantern Keepers

There were nights when the dark felt endless,
when the wind clawed at my flame,
threatening to smother all I had built.

But then, one by one,
the lanterns appeared—
not blinding, but constant,
an unfaltering radiance pooling through the dark.

Each keeper carried a fire born of resilience,
a glow kindled from personal storms.

Their hands were weathered—
knuckles traced with stories,
palms lined with memories
of holding on.

One held the fragrance of soil freshly awakened by rain,
another, spices drifting from a kitchen at dawn.
Some whispered songs older than my name;
others hummed prayers carried from distant shores.

They passed the flame,
palm to palm,
a chain of brilliance stretching across the night,
each spark igniting hope within shadows.

The beauty was not in any single lantern,
it was the way they danced together—
a constellation of courage,
a chorus of steady hands
refusing to surrender to darkness.

And now—
I carry an ember of my own.

Lit by their courage,
held by their strength,
my flame honors
the hearts that guided mine.

As I lift it high,
I watch the night transform,
illuminated by the fullness of all we are together.

In this shared glow,
I am not just one light—
I am part of a blaze
that will always rise through shadows.

I honor the light I carry, nourished by those before me.

Reflection awaits on the next page. . .

The Bloom of Me

A celebration of radiance and growth

Your bloom is a celebration—each petal a testament to the truth, resilience, and gentle courage you've cultivated.

Imagine yourself as a blossoming lotus—open yet anchored, vibrant yet peaceful.

Pause now, and reflect on your present bloom:

What internal shifts or subtle victories led you here?
How has gentle persistence guided your growth?

Write thoughtfully about the experiences shaping your bloom, honoring both restful pauses and moments of emergence. Embrace the readiness you've grown into, recognizing it as a sacred part of your becoming.

Your bloom is uniquely yours—not defined solely by challenges, but by the brave authenticity of your unfolding.

Take a moment to honor yourself fully—acknowledging, accepting, and celebrating the beauty of who you are in this moment, and who you are gently becoming.

The Bloom of Me: *A Creative Space*

———◈——◈——◈———

Draw a lotus in bloom. Within each petal, write a word or short phrase that honors a personal victory, strength, or meaningful moment that has shaped your growth. Let this drawing be a colorful reflection and joyful celebration of the journey you've traveled and the person you are presently—vibrant, confident, and whole. Fill it with colors, symbols, or designs that feel true and comforting to you. This is your bloom—a beautiful reminder of how far you've come, and how much you have to celebrate.

The Breath Between Blossoms

The bloom does not stay open forever.
Even the boldest petals
draw themselves inward at dusk,
folding their brilliance close,
nestled in the hush of evening's breath.

Yet there is aliveness hidden in stillness—
a pulse murmuring in the deep,
a heartbeat humming low in the roots,
stretching, strengthening, unseen.

The winds ease their whispers,
brushing delicately across resting leaves,
while twilight drapes the earth like velvet,
holding space for restoration.

Growth is not endless unfolding.
It is the sacred rhythm of effort and ease—
knowing that even in pause,
life stirs beneath the surface.

I honor the wisdom in retreat,
the renewal in gathering light.
I, too, am allowed to withdraw—
to let my petals close peacefully,
not from fear, but in trust.

I rest in the quiet,
where breath becomes energy,
where renewal gathers like embers,
ready to ignite the next bloom.

The bloom will open again—
bright, full, and certain.

But for now,
I honor the dusk,
the breath between blossoms,
where I am whole,
even in rest.

Grateful Glow

I honor the path that carried me—
each footprint formed by intention,
soles meeting earth
molded by persistence.

I remember the storms
I passed through—

the wind
that howled through doubts,
rain
that eased my edges,
thunder
that summoned me
back to myself.

Thank you
for the illumination that guided me—
not always vivid,
yet constant,
a flicker that stayed
when I felt most alone.

I honor voices that lifted me—
my children's laughter bubbling freely,
light-bearers who spoke clarity
into uncertainty,
the resonance of my own voice,
finding itself in moments of silence.

I give thanks
for cracks that invited softness in,
for understanding revealed by ache,
for the weight I laid down
so I could move freely.

(cont.)

Thank you
for hands extended toward me,
arms ready to hold me,
presence affirming
I never walked alone.

I honor the bloom I've become—

luminous, grounded, unapologetically myself.

Gratitude flows through me like an unending river—
a glowing testament to every step,
every lesson,
every spark that brought me here.

I honor the journey.
I honor this clarity.

And I stand here—
open and unwavering,
shining with a grateful glow.

The Glow Waits Quietly

The ember gathers slowly—
deliberate as twilight,
deepening like breath.

Strength does not hurry;
it collects itself gradually,
trusting flame rises when ready.

There is no urgency here—
only faith in simmering heat
that builds without rushing,
radiance expanding gently with time.

I once believed strength
was always loud—
a blaze roaring to announce itself.

But this ember has revealed something different—
resilience can linger,
courage often whispers.

The ember remains,
a watchful guardian
holding space for blossoms yet unseen.

It does not press forward,
acknowledging instead
that readiness itself is growth.

Even in stillness,
the ember stays steady—
persistent as coals holding quiet heat.

I lean into this low-burning presence,
trusting that when the moment arrives,
its glow will rise clearly,
illuminating the path forward.

The Alchemy of Radiance

My becoming
is etched in amber—
a celestial alchemy
rising from roots
toward suns older than the sky.

Every shard of darkness,
every weighted moment,
passed through heat and pressure,
emerging luminous,
recast into something rare.

I did not simply rise;
I transmuted.

Shadow melted into sunrise,
fear softened into brilliance,
the weight of the world
refined into filaments of stars,
my petals opening beneath cosmic dust.

I am amber and sunlight,
an echo of stars
igniting vividly
long before I took form.

(cont.)

Radiance is elemental.
It is cosmic law,
inscribed in my cells,
speaking the language
of a universe
created to shine.

This is the alchemy:

to lean into heat,
to yield to pressure,
and to emerge—
not as who I once was,
but as something infinite,
gilded,
blooming again, reborn.

The Bloom Stands Certain

I no longer apologize
for the way I stretch wide—
petals unfurling like fingers,
claiming space I once believed
was never mine.

I have learned to open
without seeking permission—
edges supple yet firm,
petals silken yet strong,
fragrance sure as sunrise.

There were seasons I stayed closed,
silent beneath the earth,
afraid my unfolding might go unnoticed.
I curled inward, uncertain
if the light would reach me—
uncertain if I was enough to greet it.

But still, I grew—
slowly, intentionally,
until the moment I knew

my bloom could no longer stay hidden.

I no longer fold myself small
for shadows that ask me to shrink.
I no longer question
whether my roots belong.

(cont.) 148

I am here—
not as a whisper, nor as a shout—
but as a presence,
unfolded and fully enough.

I do not wait for a season—
I have weathered stillness,
embraced the unseen,
and now I know my time has come.

I bloom because I recognize
my light as something innate,
never needing permission to shine.

I bloom because I believe
my fullness is not a reward I must earn.

I bloom because I am—
a presence sure as sunrise,
a glow that does not dim.

I step forward, whole and unafraid.

Reflection awaits on the next page...

Living Boldly

Stepping into your radiance

Your light is an ember steady enough to illuminate your path, a truth clear enough to guide your way. To live boldly is to trust this inner glow—to step into the world fully and freely, honoring the space you naturally claim.

Close your eyes and sense your inner radiance—constant, expansive, infinite. Imagine the life waiting for you if hesitation fell away, if you allowed your essence to guide each step.

Gently complete these declarations:
If I lived boldly, I would _____.
My inner glow inspires me to _____.

Allow your answers to emerge openly, truthfully. Let them form your song of freedom, an affirmation of the brilliance you're prepared to share. Boldness is not something you must seek—it is something already within you, waiting patiently to rise.

Optional:
Write these declarations where you'll see them daily, grounding yourself in the clarity of your inner glow. Each time you read them, remember the power you carry and the radiant life awaiting your embrace.

If I lived boldly, I would

My inner glow inspires me to

Living Boldly: *A Creative Space*

———◇———◇———◇———

This is your space to imagine, explore, and celebrate the bold life uniquely yours to claim. Draw, sketch, or map your vision of boldness, using colors, shapes, and symbols that reflect your inner truth, core values, and the essence of your radiance. Include elements that illustrate how you wish to show up in the world, the joy you'll welcome, and the vibrant energy you'll embody. There are no limits here—trust your intuition, release hesitation, and freely capture the essence of your beautifully authentic self in a way that only you can create.

My light flows beyond me, touching hearts and shaping new blooms.

SACRED PHASE 5

THE
ETERNAL LOTUS
Carrying Light Beyond Blooming

Where petals touch the wind
scattering whispers of wisdom across still waters.
Honoring the legacy of light,
the seeds carried forward,
and the knowing that blooming is never only for
oneself.

Ancestral Threads

I am stitched from fibers
older than my breath—
stories spun through generations,
carried through memory,
flowing gently from one heart
to another.

Each strand holds voices,
echoes woven like soft silk—
dreams tenderly held,
resilience generously given,
hope drifting softly forward.

Their cords entwine with mine,
weaving yesterday's murmurs
into tomorrow's tapestry—
an enduring becoming.

My story is never lived alone.
It is lifted by hands
who shaped the path before me
and by those
who will follow after.

I carry their narratives onward,
adding vibrant hues to the pattern,
extending a legacy—
grateful for the strength,
the love,
and the continuity
sewn beautifully
into me.

The Mirror and the Window

I stand before the mirror,
its surface rippling with time.

At first, I see only myself—
the arch of my brow,
the curve of my lips,
shadows lingering in my eyes.

But then, they appear—
faces sculpted from memory's clay.
My granny's strength
lives in the set of my jaw;
my peepaw's laughter
hums softly in my smile.

Their hands, their voices, their dreams—
woven into the fabric
of my reflection.

You are because we were, they whisper.
We bled, we prayed,
we dreamed you into being.
Now carry us forward.

I turn from the mirror,
the weight of their presence
still warm on my shoulders,
and gaze toward the window.

Through the glass,
I see faces not yet formed—
eyes wide with wonder,
hands eager to create,
hearts poised to ascend.

(cont.) 158

They watch me—

their whispers just as clear:
We will be because you are.
Your steps will carve our paths.
Your light guides through darkness.

The mirror holds quiet echoes—
faces that shaped me,
moments tenderly held.

The window stretches open—
visions patiently waiting,
horizons inviting my light.

And here I stand between them—
a bridge, a thread,
a flame in the chain of becoming.

I breathe in their whispers,
not as weight,
but as comforting embrace—
anchoring reflection,
a guiding glow toward tomorrow.

An infinite circle of life,
reflected in my eyes,
rooted in my hands,
waiting to bloom again.

I am the bridge between the strength of my past and the promise of my future.

Reflection awaits on the next page. . .

The Rhythm of Becoming

Life moves in cycles—beginnings, endings, and the spaces in between

Each phase shapes us, carrying its own unique wisdom.

Pause here—take a deep, grounding breath, and reflect on the subtle rhythms guiding your life.

Think of a time when one chapter of your life closed and another began.

Which threads did you intentionally carry forward? What patterns started to emerge clearly?

How has this ongoing unfolding influenced who you are today?

What truths have been quietly stitched into your being—moments that seemed small but now fell woven into who you've become?

Consider the cycles you're moving through right now.

What is rising within you? What wisdom is waiting to be seen—a thread of strength a thread of strength that's been there all along?

Write what feels true in this moment. Let your words become a thread in the rhythm of your becoming.

The Rhythm of Becoming: *A Creative Space*

———◇——◇——◇———

Imagine your life as a tapestry, each thread representing phases of your journey—moments of calm, threads of challenge, patterns of growth, and soothing intervals of rest. Use this space to sketch, draw, or describe your tapestry. Let each thread, every intricate stitch, each distinct pattern reflect the quiet wisdom and strength woven into your story. Allow your imagination to unfold freely, vividly portraying the rhythm and beauty of your continuous becoming.

The Black Lotus Legacy

From the quiet depths where shadows linger,
a seed begins—
cradled in earth's gentle embrace,
surrounded by mud rich with memory,
scented with earth's silent wisdom,
weighted by the stillness of waiting.

The mud does not stifle; it nourishes.
Each grain of soil holds subtle truths,
each drop of water forms a lifeline,
every breath whispers, *Become.*

Roots do not grow alone.
They stretch downward, seeking resilience in others,
twining into an unseen web—
a silent communion of survival and hope.

In this shared embrace,
unseen strength gathers.

And then, the bloom.
It rises, not alone,
but as the echo of countless voices
carried through generations:
You can grow here.

Petals unfold—gentle, yet unyielding,
etched with the dreams of those who reached for light,
their stories traced in veins of indigo and gold.

The Black Lotus is not singular.
It stands as testament to many,
a bloom radiant and clear,
calling to those still resting in the depths:
Your journey, an unspoken prayer.
Your roots, deeply anchored.
You are never alone.

This is its legacy:
To rise from the soil,
revealing beauty birthed not solely from hardship,
but from patience, connection, and subtle resilience.
To weave fortitude through intertwined roots,
strengthening the whole.
To affirm that even in the deepest waters,
light persistently finds its path.

Ripples of Light

A single drop falls—so small,
it seems to vanish into the vastness,
yet the water remembers.

Circles widen where it lands,
each circle humming softly,
a subtle symphony spreading
across the surface of existence,
silent and profound.

Every word we speak,
every hand we hold,
deeds that quietly defy darkness,
send glimmers through infinite waters.
The light we share today
becomes the warmth
that touches someone we may never meet,
a place we may never see.

A kind word breathed into darkness,
a spark gifted to fading embers—
these become seeds of transformation.

Even the stars are echoes,
glimmers of ancient fire,
their light traveling lifetimes
to meet our gaze.

And so, we too are vessels of brilliance.
Each subtle act,
each moment of love or truth,
extends outward,
weaving invisible threads
of connection and renewal.

A smile, a prayer, a choice—
what feels fleeting is eternal.
The pond is vast,
but every ripple
carries the rhythm of our shared radiance,
a pulse that binding us together
and to the infinite.

Cycles of Becoming

The moon waxes,
then wanes,
its glow slipping into shadow—
but always, it returns,
a silver thread binding night to dawn.

The seed sinks deep into the earth,
wrapped in darkness,
forgotten by the sun.
But it never stays motionless.
It splits open,
its quiet release giving rise to roots and wings,
stretching toward a sky it has yet to touch.

The river carves its way,
wearing stone into stories,
its voice shaping the earth,
its body flowing endlessly to the sea,
only to rise as rain,
returning to the source once more.

Between each phase,
there is pause—
a breath before the light returns,
a silence before the earth stirs again.

We mirror these cycles.
We shed ourselves in fragments:
tears that water tomorrow,
laughter that echoes through time,
prayers that linger like whispers in the wind.
Every piece we leave behind
feeds the soil of what will come next.

Every ending is a beginning
disguised in new colors.
Every offering finds its way back,
a song reshaped,
a bloom reborn.

Legacy moves like water—
fluid, persistent,
the choice to continue onward,
grace in releasing,
ease in starting over.

We are the moon,
waxing and waning.
We are the seed,
returning life to soil.

We are rivers—
endlessly flowing,
shaping stone into paths,
altering landscapes subtly,
flowing ever onward,
evolving, steady.

Within every cycle,
every unfolding,
we remain whole.

In every connection, my growth deepens; together, we rise.

Reflection awaits on the next page. . .

We Rise Together

Strength flows through the bonds we share, lifting us as we lift each other

Imagine yourself standing within a circle of hands extending across generations. Each hand you touch carries unique stories, resilience, and gentle wisdom.

Reflect quietly on these questions:

How does the support from those around you deepen your feeling of belonging? In what subtle yet meaningful ways does your presence uplift and nurture others within your circle?

Allow your thoughts to unfold naturally, capturing the gentle exchange of strength and encouragement flowing between you and your community.

Remember, your presence is integral—your contributions weave into a bond of connection that is powerful, enduring, and beautifully alive.

We Rise Together: *A Creative Space*

In this space, visually represent the circle of support and connection you've envisioned. Sketch or illustrate the hands around you—capturing their strength, warmth, and diversity. Clearly include your own hand within this circle, illustrating how your presence contributes to and enhances the community around you. Allow this creative expression to become a powerful reminder of your integral role within this interconnected circle of empowerment.

A Circle of Hands

Hands upon hands,
a circle unbroken,
stretching across time like sunlight's gentle arc.

Some weathered,
etched with the lines of fields worked,
battles fought,
lives lived in quiet resilience.

Others nurturing,
cradling dreams not yet realized,
fingers tracing paths unseen.

Some are youthful,
grasping at the promise of tomorrow,
their touch light but full of wonder.

We hold each other here,
between heritage and hope.
Ancestors cradle our trembling hands
empowering us:
We stood strong,
so you could rise.

Our hands reach forward,
toward those yet to come,
fingers extended in faith.
We whisper to them:
You will grow,
and bloom beautifully.
You will carry what we leave,
but never alone.

(cont.) 174

This circle is more than hands.
It is a hymn,
a song woven in the language of touch,
a testament to connection.
It says:
We are all part of this—
the root,
the stem,
the flower.

No hand stands apart.
No journey is solitary.
In the clasp of fingers,
the light of resilience flows—
unending,
ever renewing.

Look around—you are supported.
Look ahead—you will support.

In this infinite embrace,
bound by time,
we remain connected,
stronger together.

The Eternal Lotus

The lotus begins in the depths,
rooted in the unseen,
its beauty rising from calm waters,
unsoiled by the shadows that cradle it.

A bloom shaped by the pull of water,
the passage of time,
and the gentle persistence of becoming.

Its roots twist through memory,
drawing nourishment from what lies beneath—
the wisdom of ancestors,
the resilience of those who came before.
Each petal unfolds like a story,
a testament to growth,
carrying silent stories forward.

The lotus blooms beyond itself.
Its reflection ripples outward,
a beacon mirrored in the eyes of many.

It reaches toward the sky,
its petals a map of what is possible:
rising from uncertainty,
healing in the presence of doubt,
and thriving—
even when unseen.

(cont.) 176

We are not so different.
Our roots stretch through shared histories,
intertwining beneath the surface.
Each challenge feeds our soil,
each hope fuels the bloom.
Together, we rise—not as solitary flowers,
but as a garden woven in light,
a harmony of colors and roots.

In the heart of the lotus lies the infinite—
a rhythm of growth, rest, and renewal
spinning through eternity.
It reminds us:
we are part of this flow,
yesterday's wisdom guiding today's bloom,
seeds softly nurturing possibilities.

What we leave behind will flourish
in tranquil corners of the world.
The lotus blooms,
and so do we.

We Are the Bloom

I have walked through uncertainty,
barefoot on the edges of my own becoming.
The weight of doubt pressed heavy on my chest,
and the sky felt distant,
its stars dimmed by the haze of hesitation.

I have knelt in quiet surrender,
arms wrapped around the ache of my unfolding.
Yet even in that stillness,
a seed stirred in the soil of my soul.
Each tear became rain.
each scar, a sunbeam piercing clouds.

My growth came gently
roots reaching deeper,
my petals trembling yet determined to open.
sunlight softly touching each fold.

And now, I rise.
A bloom nurtured by the wisdom of yesterday,
my petals carry the story of becoming.
But I do not rise alone.

We are not separate blooms;
we are a garden—
each flower offering something to the next,
a rhythm of mutual care and renewal.

Your moments of courage whisper strength to another.
Your quiet victories illuminate paths
for those still finding their way.

We rise not alone, but together—
a garden woven with resilience,
a tapestry stitched with resolve.

Our roots entwine beneath the surface,
hidden yet strong,
branches reaching toward endless skies.

We pause—
acknowledging that courage was found
not in standing alone,
but in leaning gently into one another.

Our petals catch the light
and pass it on,
turning shadows
into sanctuaries of growth.

We embody the bloom.
We become the legacy.
We sustain the radiance,
lifting each other higher,
toward horizons
where the garden endlessly thrives.

My bloom carries more than my own story—
I hold the warmth of hands that guided me,
their steady light flickering forward.

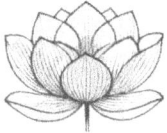

Our bloom is not the end—it is the beginning of what we pass forward.

Reflection awaits on the next page. . .

What You Leave Behind

Seeds of legacy, gardens of tomorrow

Take a peaceful moment to reflect on the lasting impact you're creating—like lotus seeds intentionally placed in nurturing mud, patiently awaiting their graceful bloom.

Consider deeply:

What legacy of love, authenticity, or bravery do you feel inspired to cultivate? Whose lives—both known to you and those beyond your sight—will be illuminated by the way you choose to live?

Envision your intentions gently unfolding through generations, your actions like seeds slowly blossoming into guidance, comfort, and inspiration long after you have passed your light onward.

Write from the heart, embracing the vision of your impact extending gently outward, growing into a flourishing garden of wisdom, beauty, and profound connection.

What You Leave Behind: *A Creative Space*

Visualize your life as a garden, where each action, word, and choice becomes a seed for the future. What do you imagine growing there? Use this space to express your vision—describe the blooms, draw their shapes, or write about the ways your garden might nourish and inspire others. Let your creativity reflect the legacy you are cultivating.

The Legacy of Light

Bearer of light
know this:
your journey matters profoundly.
Each stride forward,
each spark ignited,
each truth spoken
sends ripples into the universe.

You may not see the seeds you've planted,
but they will grow—
in the hearts of those who follow,
in spaces your touch may never reach.

Your glow transcends your own being,
a beacon amidst shadows,
a luminous thread stitched into the fabric of eternity.

Even when the night feels endless,
when your flame wavers,
remember—
you belong to an expansive galaxy,
a symphony of starlight
resonating across lifetimes.

What you give today
will rise as the dawn for someone else.
What you heal now
builds havens for futures unknown.

You are a legacy,
a bridge between what was and what will be.
Hold your radiance intentionally,
with unwavering grace,
with devoted love,
trusting its lasting impact.

When your hands are still,
when your voice softens into cherished memory,
your light persists
engraved in the lives you've brightened,
in dreams you've inspired,
in worlds you've transformed.

I carry my ember forward—
not just for me,
but for those who will follow—
a promise that glows beyond the horizon,
burning steady and sure.

The Torchbearer's Song

They sat by the fire,
its glow casting long shadows,
each flicker an unspoken story.

The child leaned close, eyes wide,
a vessel waiting to be filled with light.

Once, I walked through shadows,
the voice began, low and steady,
feet bare against the weight of silence,
heart heavy by the unseen.
The world tried to quiet me,
but my voice grew roots.
My song became my light,
and I learned to carry it.

The child reached toward the flame,
fingers tracing its boundary,
feeling its warmth without touch.
What did you do when the light dimmed? they asked.

I held it near, the voice replied,
shielded it gently with my breath,
wrapped it softly in my tears.
I fed it with the whispers of ancestors,
their songs curling like smoke through the dark—
soft yet steady, rising with me.

The flame was never mine alone,
but thrived because of me.

The fire cracked,
its sparks leaping like stars into the dark.
The figure turned,
their gaze unwavering, their voice clear:

(cont.) 186

Now it is your turn.
This torch is ancient,
carried by hands that bled and healed,
kept alive by hearts unwilling to break.

Hold it high,
so others may find their way.
Keep it close,
so it may guide you, too.
Nourish it with love,
and it will never fade.

Their heart trembled,
yet courage rose quietly,
meeting the flame with trust.

It leapt to their palm—
not scorching, but filling them with warmth,
a light so deep it seemed to sing.

I will carry it, they whispered,
their voice gentle, but curtain.
A smile shimmered in the shadows,
blending with the stars above.

And someday, the voice said,
you will pass it on.

The fire burned on,
ancient, eternal,
its song passed forward,
a melody of light
woven into the fabric of time.

And still, that flame moves—
glowing quietly in others,
waiting to be kindled once more.

I cherish who I am and trust who I am becoming.

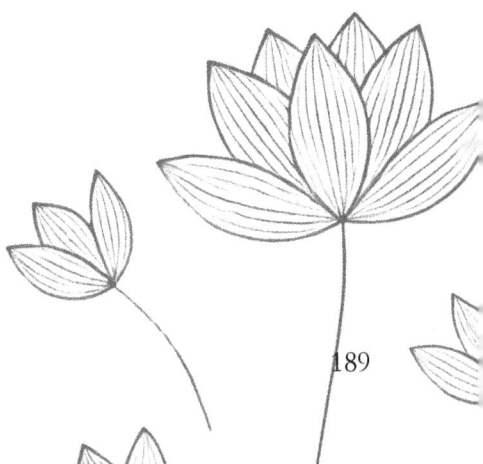

THE ETERNAL GARDEN

A Haven for Ongoing Reflection and Growth

The journey you've experienced in *Sacred Black Bloom* does not end with these pages—it continues within you.

Each reflection, each breath, and each still moment you've embraced becomes part of your ongoing growth. As you move forward, know that this book will always hold space for you to return, reflect, and reconnect.

The Eternal Garden is a poetic space where we exhale deeply, tend compassionately, and bloom again and again—rooted in the heart of Sacred Black Bloom. Here, there is no rush or final form, only intentional moments of pause and mindful reflection. You'll receive occasional offerings—seasonal insights, poetic musings, and heartfelt affirmations—each one shared when the soil is ripe, no sooner, no later.

Visit **sacredblackbloom.com** or scan below to step into this digital garden and receive your welcoming collection, *Petals of Becoming*—affirmations and reflections thoughtfully offered to support your continual blooming.

Your journey is ever-deepening.
Your bloom is continuous.
You are always welcome here.

Closing reflections await you on the next pages.

Reflecting on My Bloom

Witnessing my bloom with love and grace

Pause here, taking a moment to honor yourself and the journey you've embraced throughout these pages.

These reflections will lovingly guide you in:

Honoring Your Journey – recognizing the steps you've taken and the strength you've gathered.

Celebrating Your Truth – embracing the authenticity you've discovered about yourself.

Peace and Gratitude – finding joy and gratitude in the experiences that shaped you.

A Gentle Promise – making a compassionate commitment to yourself for the future.

Moving Forward With Love – carrying your journey forward with kindness and compassion.

Reflect thoughtfully and openly, allowing yourself to fully appreciate the unique and beautiful growth you've experienced.

Honoring Your Journey

What have I discovered about myself that I want to remember always?

In what ways have I shown courage, kindness, or honesty during my growth?

Celebrating Your Truth

What truths do I now embrace about who I am, and how does accepting these truths bring me peace?

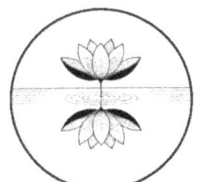

Peace and Gratitude

What moments from this journey am I truly grateful for, and how will I carry their warmth forward?

A Gentle Promise

What promise can I gently make to myself to keep honoring the growth and wisdom I've gathered?

Moving Forward With Love

As I move forward, how will I continue to hold space for my story, treating myself with compassion and love?

A Note of Gratitude

With a heart deep in gratitude, I honor you. Thank you for sharing this sacred space with me—your presence, your courage, and your openness are seen and deeply valued.

Sacred Black Bloom was born because the journey of becoming deserves to be recognized, celebrated, and embraced in all its complexities. These words honor moments of stillness, the courage found in vulnerability, the strength discovered through trust, and the steady rhythm of growth. They acknowledge every step you've taken—no matter how small or unseen—as an essential thread in your beautifully unfolding story.

This offering is my acknowledgment of the many voices that have spoken life into me, those who reminded me of my own light so that I could, in turn, remind you of yours. It is my hope that these pages have gently encouraged you to trust your own rhythms, to pause when needed, and to rise when ready.

Thank you for allowing these words to walk alongside you, reminding you of your innate worth and infinite potential. May gratitude continue to guide your path, and may your bloom be forever luminous, rooted deeply in love and authenticity.

With endless love and appreciation,

Jasmine L. Smith
Author of *Sacred Black Bloom*